Awesome Ghosts of Ontario

by Catherine Pelonero

Single copies of plays are sold for reading purposes only. The copying or duplicating of a play, or any part of a play, by hand or by any other process, is an infringement of the copyright. Such infringement will be vigorously prosecuted.

Baker's Plays
7611 Sunset Blvd.
Los Angeles, CA 90042
bakersplays.com

NOTICE

This book is offered for sale at the price quoted only on the understanding that, if any additional copies of the whole or any part are necessary for its production, such additional copies will be purchased. The attention of all purchasers is directed to the following: this work is fully protected under the copyright laws of the United States of America, the British Commonwealth, including Canada, and all other countries of the Copyright Union. Violations of the Copyright Law are punishable by fine or imprisonment, or both. The copying or duplication of this work or any part of this work, by hand or by any process, is an infringement of the copyright and will be vigorously prosecuted.

This play may not be produced by amateurs or professionals for public or private performance without first submitting application for performing rights. Royalties are due on all performances whether for charity or gain, or whether admission is charged or not. Since performance of this play without the payment of the royalty fee renders anybody participating liable to severe penalties imposed by the law, anybody acting in this play should be sure, before doing so, that the royalty fee has been paid. Professional rights, reading rights, radio broadcasting, television and all mechanical rights, etc. are strictly reserved. Application for performing rights should be made directly to BAKER'S PLAYS.

No one shall commit or authorize any act or omission by which the copyright of, or the right to copyright, this play may be impaired. No one shall make any changes in this play for the purpose of production.

Publication of this play does not imply availability for performance. Both amateurs and professionals considering a production are strongly advised in their own interest to apply to Baker's Plays for written permission before starting rehearsals, advertising, or booking a theatre.

Whenever the play is produced, the author's name must be carried in all publicity, advertising and programs. Also, the following notice must appear on all printed programs, "Produced by special arrangement with Baker's Plays."

Licensing fees for AWESOME GHOSTS OF ONTARIO are based on a per performance rate and payable one week in advance of the production.

Please consult the Baker's Plays website at www.bakersplays.com or our current print catalogue for up to date licensing fee information.

Copyright © 2010 by Catherine Pelonero
Made in U.S.A.
All rights reserved.

AWESOME GHOSTS OF ONTARIO
ISBN **978-0-87440-235-3**
#2050-B

AWESOME GHOSTS OF ONTARIO was first produced by Regina Little Theatre, Regina, Saskatchewan (Nora Berg, Artistic Director; Angel Genereux, Producer) on April 25, 2008. The lighting and sound design was by Lyle McMillan, costume design by Sandra Andersen, hair and makeup by Kathy Neal and Darcy Wilson. The stage manager was Erin Missick, assistant stage manager was Scott Letourneau. Kevin Rispler directed the following cast:

ALICE . . . . Valeria Doiron
JESSIE . . . . Chelsa Reil
EVAN . . . . Mathieu Langlois
HANNAH . . . . .Samantha Workman
GROVER . . . . Josh Peter

DRAMATIS PERSONAE

ALICE – She's about 19. Enthusiastic, driven, energetic, and very sincere in her aims.

JESSIE – She's about 17. Smart and witty. Sarcastic but not mean-spirited.

EVAN – He's about 19. An easygoing guy who's game for adventure, though he's burned out on this one.

HANNAH – Late teens to early 20s. Cheerful and oblivious. She's in her own world and happy to be there.

GROVER – In his early 20s. A regular guy out for a day of deer hunting.

There is some flexibility here with the ages of the characters. Alice, Jessie and Evan should be somewhere in their late teens. Hannah and Grover could be teenagers or a little older, though under 30 probably works best.

SCENE

A clearing in deep woods in rural Ontario, Canada.

TIME

A Saturday in early October.

*This play is dedicated to anyone who ever ordered
a large coffee at the Tim Hortons drive-through
and to my niece Breanna, with love*

(*SETTING: A clearing in deep woods somewhere outside Toronto.*)

(*AT RISE:* **ALICE**, *dressed for chilly weather and wearing a bright orange vest, steps into the stage area and looks around with growing excitement. Standing center, she closes her eyes, takes a deep breath and holds both her arms out, hands cupped, in a meditative stance. She takes another deep breath. Her eyes snap open. She smiles.*)

ALICE. (*overjoyed*) This is perfect. This is *perfect*!

(*calling off*)

Come on, I found a great spot! Hurry up!

(**ALICE** *rushes around as if surveying the area, assessing the light, etc.*)

ALICE. (*cont.*) (*to herself*) Okay, I can stand right here… this light through the trees is good…awesome background…

(*calling off*)

Guys, hurry up! Let's go!

JESSIE. (*offstage*) I'm coming, I'm coming…

(**JESSIE** *enters. She is also dressed warmly with some sort of bright orange vest over her jacket and a camera bag slung over one shoulder. In contrast to* **ALICE**'*s excited energy,* **JESSIE** *shuffles on, feet dragging, looking exhausted and like she'd rather be anywhere else in the world but here.*)

ALICE. (*arms open wide*) Check this out…isn't it great?! Isn't this the perfect location?

(**JESSIE** *plops down on a log, lets out a big sigh.*)

JESSIE. Yeah. Great.

ALICE. The energy in this clearing is phenomenal, it's just pouring out everywhere! Can't you feel it? Can't you just feel the energy here?

JESSIE. *(snappishly)* I can't even feel my own toes!

ALICE. What's wrong with you?

JESSIE. Alice, don't take this the wrong way, but I hate you.

ALICE. Don't be a baby! I brought you out here because I thought you were tough.

JESSIE. *Tough?* You don't have to be tough to wander around the woods for hours, you just have to have absolutely nothing else going on in your life!

ALICE. I told you this would be hard work.

JESSIE. You told me that if I helped you out, you'd help *me* learn to drive, and that's the only reason I'm here. Remember, two hours of driving lessons for every one hour I'm forced to follow you through the forest.

ALICE. Yeah, yeah. Hand me the camera.

JESSIE. Because if I don't get my driver's license out of this…

ALICE. Hand me the camera.

JESSIE. *(as she hands over camera bag)* I mean it, Alice. If you don't keep your promise I'll never speak to you again! And I'll tell Mom.

ALICE. *(mocking) I'll tell Mom, I'll tell Mom…*Are you a teenager or a toddler?

JESSIE. I'm tired! And I have blisters the size of pancakes!

(**ALICE** *has removed a camcorder from the bag and makes adjustments on it during the following.*)

ALICE. Quit whining! And listen, Jessie, you're out here as my associate, not my little sister, so be a professional and don't threaten me with Mom. You want credit on the project, don't you? Don't you want to see your name up on screen?

JESSIE. I'd rather see my feet in a hot bath.

ALICE. *(looking off)* What happened to Evan and Hannah? Where are they?

JESSIE. Probably driving back to Toronto as fast as they can.
ALICE. Weren't they right behind you?
JESSIE. They were. Evan kept tripping and dropping stuff.
ALICE. Dropping stuff? Jessie! Why didn't you help him?
JESSIE. Why didn't *you*?
ALICE. I can't scout locations if I'm weighed down with equipment, can I? You should have helped him. I swear, if any of that gear is damaged...
JESSIE. What? You'll fire me and find a new sister?

(From offstage, a heavy thud and loud cries of pain: Oww! Oh man give me a break, OWWWW!*)*

ALICE. That must be Evan.
JESSIE. Either that or a talking elk just fell over a log.

*(**EVAN** enters, groaning and angry and looking disheveled. Wearing an orange vest and bright orange hat, he also carries numerous bags and backpacks slung over his shoulders, around his neck, and anywhere else possible.)*

ALICE. *(brightly)* Hey Evan!
EVAN. *(with a scowl)* Don't talk to me.

(collapsing on the ground)

Alice, nothing personal, but I hate you.

ALICE. Where's Hannah?
EVAN. Over there. She's looking for berries.
ALICE. Berries! What kind of berries does she think she'll find in early October?
EVAN. How should I know? She's *your* cousin.
JESSIE. *(to **ALICE**)* You know Hannah's not the sharpest tool in the shed.

*(about **ALICE**, sotto voce)*

Not that everyone on our side of the family is a genius.

ALICE. Well I'm not waiting for her. There's no telling how long this energy field will last. Jess, give me a hand.

(EVAN is lying flat on his back. ALICE starts removing items from the packs that are still attached to him as he lies there trying to catch his breath. JESSIE remains seated on the log.)

ALICE. *(with excitement)* I knew we were on the right track. All the way up here I felt like we were heading toward something, you know?

EVAN. Something dead.

ALICE. Well of course, all spirits are deceased people.

EVAN. No, I mean that smell; all the way up the trail there was a nasty smell.

JESSIE. You're right! I smelled it too. It was like garbage mixed with a wet dog and a corpse.

EVAN. Speaking of corpses, can somebody explain the logic of us being so deep in the woods during hunting season?

ALICE. Don't worry about it, we're wearing orange. Besides, it's too early in the season, there probably aren't any hunters out yet.

EVAN & JESSIE. Yeah, right!

JESSIE. Hey, they don't give hunting licenses to people who are color-blind, do they? I mean what if there's some color-blind guy out here with a rifle?

EVAN. *(still huffing and puffing)* He can shoot me. Put me out of my misery, please. In fact, hand me a couple branches I can tie on my head to look like antlers.

ALICE. What a couple of crybabies you are! A little bit of hiking through the woods…

EVAN. Little bit of hiking?! This is the third time we've driven out to the middle of nowhere. A couple more days of this and I'll turn feral.

ALICE. Scientific research takes time.

JESSIE. A movie about ghosts. That's real scientific, Alice.

ALICE. I told you a hundred times it is *not* a movie; it is a Multimedia Documentary! And it's going to be awesome. We're in the right place, I know it. We're going to catch some great sound and video.

EVAN. I hope you're right. I think the only thing we're gonna catch out here is Lyme disease.

ALICE. We have to keep our eyes and minds open and we'll see something.

JESSIE. Aw, Alice, all we've seen so far is a moose, a pile of beef jerky wrappers, and a woodchuck that stole my bag of grapes.

ALICE. If the two of you would stop complaining and *concentrate*, you'd sense that there's a disturbance in the life force in this area.

JESSIE. *(rolling her eyes)* Whatever, Yoda. The only disturbance around here is us, sitting around in these stupid orange vests!

ALICE. We look like experienced outdoor people.

JESSIE. We look like a bunch of deranged crossing guards.

ALICE. Jessie…someday when I'm one of the world's foremost paranormal investigators, you're going to be sorry.

JESSIE. Yeah, sorry that we have the same last name.

(Gunfire in the distance. **EVAN** *pops his head up in alarm.)*

EVAN. What was that? Was that gunshots?

ALICE. Don't worry about it. It's probably 100 kilometers away. Besides, it's probably just a car backfiring or something.

EVAN. *(to* **JESSIE***)* She has an optimistic answer for everything.

*(***ALICE** *has laid out her gear: a thermometer, shoebox, microphone, director's clapboard, notebook and a small hand-held device which she proudly holds up.)*

ALICE. Here it is…*the* most valuable tool in the search for paranormal activity.

EVAN. An iPod?

ALICE. No! This is my EMF. My electromagnetic field detector.

EVAN. Oh, that thing.

ALICE. This isn't a *thing*, it's a highly specialized piece of technology. A tri-field meter with a squelch mechanism. The kind used by all true professionals, not just some cheap gadget...

JESSIE. Yeah we know, you slaved away for a year at Tim Hortons to save up the money, blah blah blah.

(**ALICE** *gives* **JESSIE** *a dirty look. She shoves the EMF detector in her pocket, grabs the clapboard and heads back toward the center area.*)

ALICE. All right, let's shoot the intro. Jessie, grab the camera.

(**JESSIE** *grudgingly takes the camcorder and follows* **ALICE.**)

ALICE. Okay, stand right there and get me in frame. Evan, stop breathing.

EVAN. Excuse me?

ALICE. Stop panting! You sound like a Labrador retriever!

EVAN. I carry all this junk up here for you like I'm your personal pack mule and now I'm not even allowed to breathe?

ALICE. Just keep it quiet for a minute. Jessie, have you got me in frame?

JESSIE. *(dully)* Yes.

ALICE. Come on, Jessie, show a little enthusiasm.

JESSIE. Yay! A multimedia documentary, yay! The woods are haunted, yay!!!!

(**EVAN** *giggles.* **ALICE** *stares angrily at* **JESSIE.**)

ALICE. Do *I* make fun of *your* goals and ambitions, Jessie? Did I laugh when you wanted to build a tree house just like the one on *Mr. Dressup*?

JESSIE. Oh that was only like a thousand years ago, Alice!

ALICE. *(mocking)* Please, Alice, oh please help me write a letter to Chester the Crow...

JESSIE. I never said that!

EVAN. Fight about it later, sisters, I can only hold my breath for so long.

(props up on his elbows)

Hey, should we look for Hannah? Make sure she knows where we are?

ALICE. No, she'll turn up. If she's as in-touch with the spirit world as she says, she'll be drawn to this spot anyway. Okay; let's do this.

*(**ALICE** takes a deep breath. She straightens up and assumes what she thinks is her most austere pose for the camera. She holds the clapboard up in front of her.)*

ALICE. Ready? Roll camera! Awesome Ghosts of Ontario, introduction, take one.

*(Snaps the clapboard, tosses it aside, and clears her throat. Looking directly at the camera, she speaks the following in the halting, measuredly emphatic manner of a newsmagazine correspondent. Though her delivery comes off as overdone and humorous, **ALICE** is very sincere.)*

Ghosts. Spirits. Unexplained voices. Are they real, or imaginary? Friends, or foes? Good…or evil?

(A dramatic pause; she moves around the area.)

When most of us think of hauntings, we think of haunted houses, hotels, lighthouses…But the spirit world is not limited to dusty old buildings.

(indicating the scenery)

The beautiful wilderness of Ontario can be home to many things…Bears, elk, deer, raccoons. And also…to Ghosts. Join us on our quest as we investigate, the Awesome Ghosts of Ontario. I'm Alice Wimbley.

(a look for the camera, then:)

Cut!

*(to **EVAN** and **JESSIE**)*

How was that? Was it okay?

(They thought it was over-the-top, but they want to be nice.)

JESSIE. It was good.

ALICE. Really?

(JESSIE and EVAN nod and smile.)

EVAN. *(kindly)* You sounded very serious.

ALICE. *(smiling)* Thanks! I have to be serious, if I'm not I can't expect my audience to be. Some people think that hauntings are just a big joke. Well, to all the skeptics I want to say, watch *this*, and *then* we'll see if you're still laughing!

(JESSIE and EVAN exchange a look which ALICE doesn't notice, as she is already preparing for the next shot.)

ALICE. Okay, let's change position. I'll stand over here and Jessie, you shoot from over there. Okay; quiet on the set...

EVAN. Hey...it is really quiet. Have you noticed that? I mean it seems extra quiet around here. I don't even hear the usual forest sounds. Not even a squirrel.

ALICE. Never mind the squirrels! We have work to do.

EVAN. All right, all right!

ALICE. Ready, Jessie?

JESSIE. Ready.

ALICE. Roll camera!

(assuming her correspondent voice)

The sounds of spirits are often more mystifying than the sight of them. On a still, quiet day in the right location, it is possible to record Electronic Voice Phenomena, or EVPs – unexplained spoken words or voices...Talking heard when no person is talking. At least, no *living* person.

(brief pause for effect)

Where do these voices come from? What do the spirits beyond want to tell us?

(from offstage in the distance, **HANNAH***'s voice, yelling:)*

HANNAH. I need to use the bathroom!

ALICE. Cut!

HANNAH. *(offstage)* Yoo-hoo!

JESSIE. Over here, Hannah.

*(***HANNAH*** enters, bottle of spring water in hand. Aside from her footwear,* **HANNAH** *looks like she's dressed more for a club than for the woods. Her coat and clothes are stylish – perhaps too stylish – her hair and makeup done, plenty of jewelry. Happy and nonchalant, she steps into the clearing as if she's stepping into a cocktail party.)*

HANNAH. Hello!

ALICE. Hello! Thanks for ruining that shot, Hannah!

HANNAH. *(oblivious)* Shot? What shot? I didn't hear a thing.

JESSIE. How'd the berry picking work out for you?

HANNAH. Oh disastrous! I didn't find one and I'm totally starving! I need to use a bathroom too. Where is it?

EVAN. Pick a tree.

HANNAH. Evan, don't be barbaric. Really, where is the bathroom?

JESSIE. Hannah, are you kidding? There are no bathrooms out here.

HANNAH. No? Hmm. Well, I suppose I'll have to wait then. Thank goodness for the power of mind over matter.

ALICE. Where's your orange vest?

HANNAH. I gave it to a deer.

ALICE. What?!

HANNAH. Yes, there was a doe back there and she was so sweet. I put it on her.

EVAN. You lie! No deer would let you get close enough.

HANNAH. No deer would let *you* get close enough, darling. I have a special connection with nature.

ALICE. You have to wear orange, Hannah.

HANNAH. I look terrible in orange!

ALICE. It's a safety thing, not a fashion statement.

HANNAH. Don't be silly, I'm perfectly safe. Nobody's going to shoot me. I haven't done anything. Now, how about a bite to eat?

ALICE. *(with a sigh, motions to bags around* **EVAN***)* Over there. Just a quick snack, okay, because we've got stuff to do.

*(***HANNAH*** kneels down by ***EVAN***, who is sitting, and she rummages through the bags.)*

JESSIE. *(to* **ALICE***)* I'm hungry too.

ALICE. Fine. All of you have a snack, I'll set up the microphone so we can record EVPs.

JESSIE. Great, you do that.

*(***JESSIE*** joins ***EVAN*** and ***HANNAH***, who is pulling out little bags of snack food that the three of them munch on during the following while ***ALICE*** sets up the microphone, writes in her notebook, etc.)*

HANNAH. Alice, you didn't happen to bring any apple fritters from Hortons, did you?

ALICE. *(coldly)* No, I didn't. I'm only an employee there, not a customer.

HANNAH. No?

JESSIE. *(to* **HANNAH***, sotto voce)* Don't get her started…

ALICE. *(bitter indignation)* They laugh at me at Tim Hortons.

HANNAH. The apple fritters laugh at you?

ALICE. My ignorant, narrow-minded co-workers. "Alice is a ghost hunter, ha ha! Hey Alice, there's a tray of Dutchies missing, do you think a ghost stole them? Ha ha!"

HANNAH. Oh, what a shame. You'd think they'd screen their employees a little better.

ALICE. Nobody at Tim Hortons believes me. They don't believe that I've actually recorded paranormal voices. I showed them a picture I took at a house in Burlington which clearly shows an orb and they all said it was probably just a dust ball.

HANNAH. There's a haunted Tim Hortons in Nova Scotia, you know.

ALICE. *(interested)* Really?

HANNAH. Oh yes! I know somebody who used to work there. The coffee maker would turn on by itself and boxes of Timbits would fly off the shelves.

ALICE. Has anyone investigated?

EVAN. *(to ALICE)* Before you even suggest it, I am not driving out to Nova Scotia so you can investigate a haunted Hortons.

ALICE. I wouldn't suggest it *now*. I don't want ghosts in Nova Scotia in my documentary about ghosts of Ontario. Duh!

HANNAH. You may want to keep it in mind for the future. It's a real hot spot.

JESSIE. I'll bet. Flying Timbits.

ALICE. *(considering)* You know, I bet if we drove in shifts we could make it there in a day and a half.

EVAN. Count me out!

JESSIE. I could help with the driving. After I get my *driver's license*, of course!

HANNAH. *(looking in a bag)* Jessie, didn't you bring some grapes?

JESSIE. Gone. Woodchuck stole 'em.

EVAN. That woodchuck didn't steal your grapes.

JESSIE. The grapes were on a log, a woodchuck sat next to the log. I turn away for a second and when I turn back, the grapes and the woodchuck are both gone.

EVAN. Yeah, but I don't think a woodchuck would do that.

HANNAH. Oh you'd be amazed at what a woodchuck will do. My brother's friend Gordy had a pet woodchuck. His name was Francis and he could open beer cans.

EVAN. No way!

JESSIE. Did he drink the beer?

HANNAH. Unfortunately he did, and it put him on a tragic path.

JESSIE. What do you mean? Like the woodchuck would stagger around and beg for change at drive-throughs and stuff?

(**EVAN** and **JESSIE** *laugh but* **HANNAH** *continues unperturbed, meaning every word she says.*)

HANNAH. No, nothing like that, but a terrible accident lead to his death. One day he had one too many – and you know, for a woodchuck even one Labatts is too many – and he fell in front of a Zamboni. And that was the end of Francis. Of course it was Gordy's fault. Drunk or sober, you should never take a woodchuck to hockey practice. I mean that's just common sense, right?

(**EVAN** *and* **JESSIE** *stare at her, dumbfounded.*)

ALICE. Hannah, can you come here for a minute?

HANNAH. Sure!

(**HANNAH** *approaches* **ALICE.**)

ALICE. *(to* **HANNAH***)* Do you sense an anomaly in this area?

(**HANNAH** *looks around, nods slowly.*)

HANNAH. I do. There's a little tingling feeling in my gums, you know? That only happens when either there's an otherworldly presence or when I drink too much Clamato.

(**EVAN** *turns to* **JESSIE.**)

EVAN. So, are you the only sane one in your family?

JESSIE. Pretty much.

ALICE. Jessie, Evan, I need both of you.

(**JESSIE** *and* **EVAN** *rise and lumber over.*)

EVAN. Alice, do you think maybe we could start heading home pretty soon, maybe find some indoor ghosts for your documentary?

ALICE. I don't want indoor ghosts! All the indoor ghosts are taken.

EVAN. Taken?

ALICE. Just about every haunted building has already been investigated…

HANNAH. Except the Tim Hortons in Nova Scotia.

ALICE. I want to give the undiscovered, lesser known spirits a chance.

EVAN. A chance to what?

ALICE. You know, communicate with us. Besides, Hannah's encounter with a ghost happened in the woods so I want her to tell her story in an outdoor setting.

*(**ALICE** heads over to the bags to retrieve something.)*

JESSIE. *(to **HANNAH**)* Do you really think you've seen ghosts or are you just playing with her?

HANNAH. Oh, I *know* I've seen ghosts. There's no doubt. Well, let me be clear; I have seen one ghost, I've heard and sensed many others, and one I'm related to personally. Yes, my great Uncle Ron. He was on the other side of the family, not your side. I've never seen him myself but I've had several very reliable sources tell me that he regularly haunts a stretch of road outside of Hamilton. I wish I could make contact with him. Poor thing, he's a very tormented soul.

EVAN. How do you know?

HANNAH. Well he died so suddenly and violently. Niagara Falls. He went right over the Falls.

JESSIE. Seriously? He fell in the river?

HANNAH. No, he was a daredevil. He was trying to go over the Falls in a barrel.

JESSIE. Oh my God!

HANNAH. Yes. He was a great stunt man but unfortunately he wasn't a detail oriented kind of guy. He forgot to put the lid on the barrel before he went into the river. And, you know, it just didn't work out.

EVAN. So if he died violently at Niagara Falls, why doesn't he haunt the Falls?

HANNAH. Oh he never really liked it there. Too many tourists.

(**ALICE** *returns.*)

ALICE. Evan, you take the thermometer...

(hands him a large outdoor type thermometer)

Walk slowly around that area up there and let me know of any sudden temperature changes because that can signal a paranormal event. Jessie, you're going to hold the tape recorder...

(hands her a shoebox)

Whatever you do, *don't* take the tape recorder out of the shoebox.

JESSIE. *(dull sarcasm)* Okay, I'll try not to.

ALICE. *(to no one in particular)* See, the recorder is in the box wrapped in a towel. We extend the microphone as far away from it as possible and it cuts down on the recorder noise when we're taping EVPs.

HANNAH. Oh, good thinking!

ALICE. *(with her EMF detector in hand)* And I am going to test the EMF...

*(She points the device at **JESSIE**. It makes a steady beeping sound.)*

ALICE. See that? It's picking you up. It only measures natural energy.

JESSIE. *(wryly)* Wonderful.

*(**ALICE** points it away from **JESSIE** and beeping stops. She points it offstage, waving it steadily back and forth as she steps forward.)*

ALICE. Hold your positions...I'll be right back...!

*(**ALICE** walks off waving the EMF in front of her. **HANNAH** turns to **EVAN** and **JESSIE**, who look glum and bored.)*

HANNAH. *(with a smile)* I suppose you're both dying to hear about the time I actually saw a ghost.

JESSIE. Not really.

EVAN. No.

HANNAH. *(as if they answered "Yes, please!")* It was in woods just like these. About three or ten years ago. I was standing by some blueberry bushes when suddenly I felt a chill. I turned and there he was, not more than a stone's throw away. He stepped right out in front of me, he did!

EVAN. Who did?

HANNAH. It was the figure of a man. I mean he was kind of misty but you could definitely tell it was a man. He had gray hair and glasses and he was wearing this very, very bright, flamboyant suit, and it looked to me like he wanted to say something, like he was desperate to speak.

EVAN. You sure it wasn't just Don Cherry out moose hunting?

HANNAH. Evan, what a skeptic you are. Why did you come on a ghost hunt?

EVAN. *(shrugs)* I thought it would be cool.

HANNAH. And?

EVAN. It's not.

*(**ALICE** returns.)*

ALICE. Okay, I double-checked the area and we're not near any power or water lines so we shouldn't get any false energy readings.

*(handing EMF to **HANNAH**)*

Hannah, hold this but keep it pointed away for now. Jess, bring the tape recorder over here.

*(**JESSIE** follows **ALICE** to an upstage area. **ALICE** has taken a long cord from her pocket. She attaches one end presumably to the tape recorder in the shoebox and extends the cord a distance to attach the other end to the microphone.)*

EVAN. *(looking around, a little nervous)* I can't get over how quiet it is here. It's kind of eerie.

ALICE. What's eerie about it? It's perfect for recording EVPs!

EVAN. Yeah, well, those of us who aren't in tune with the spirit world have a different take on it.

JESSIE. What do you mean?

EVAN. When the woods get really silent like this, I mean when all the birds and animals hide and stay quiet, it can mean there's a large predator in the area.

HANNAH. There *are* large predators in the area, darling. That would be us.

JESSIE. Yeah, that's it; the animals are probably just scared of us.

(EVAN looks around, slowly shakes his head.)

EVAN. No…I don't think that's it.

JESSIE. Are you trying to scare us?

EVAN. No, I'm just trying to be cautious.

ALICE. Don't worry about it. Jess, go as far as you can without pulling the cord out and find a stable place to put the recorder.

(JESSIE moves to an upstage area and sets the shoebox down. Her nose wrinkles and she makes a face.)

JESSIE. Euwww…it smells over here.

EVAN. *(sniffing the air)* It's back again. That bad smell.

HANNAH. There is an odor here, isn't there?

EVAN. Where the heck is that coming from?

ALICE. *(ignoring their comments)* Now what we're going to do is –

(ALICE is cut off abruptly as the EMF in HANNAH's hand starts to beep rapidly.)

ALICE. *(to HANNAH)* What did you do?

HANNAH. Nothing, I'm just standing here like you told me.

(Suddenly they begin to hear noise in the distance, as if something large was running through the woods. They all freeze.)

JESSIE. *(frightened whisper)* What is that?

EVAN. *(equally scared)* I don't know, but it's heading right toward us!

HANNAH. *(excited)* I wonder if it's the spirit of my Uncle Ron. He loved to run!

ALICE. Shhhhh!

*(The EMF beeps louder and faster as the sound of something crashing through the woods gets closer. They hear panting. Suddenly a man bursts into the clearing, out of breath and clearly scared to death. This is **GROVER**, dressed in hunting garb: blaze orange pants, white long sleeved thermal shirt and a hunting hat with flaps. He collapses to his knees and tries to speak but he is too panicked and out of breath for the words to make sense.)*

GROVER. I was…he…I saw…huge! Huge! Ohhhh! Uhhhh! Ahhhh!

*(They watch him, too stunned to react. **GROVER** motions to them and continues to babble.)*

GROVER. Wuh…wa…water! Water! Please…

*(**JESSIE** hands a water bottle to **GROVER**, who grabs it and drinks. He begins to calm down and regain his composure.)*

GROVER. Thank you. Thank you! Oh thank God you're here!

HANNAH. Is something wrong?

*(**GROVER** nods. He gets back on his feet. Panting and agitated, he launches into his story at a frantic pace.)*

GROVER. So I'm in my tree stand. I got my thirty-oh-six pointed at the greatest eight point buck I've ever seen when I smell this *god-awful* stink. I can barely hold my rifle straight cause this odor is making my eyes water. I see something in the bush…I'm thinking it's Dennis – my buddy, you don't know him – cause Dennis is always turning up where he's least wanted, right? Then this thing stands up and it's *not* Dennis…it's huge, it's hairy and it's walking on two legs.

(brief pause)

GROVER. *(cont.)* Sasquatch. Bigfoot! I swear to God! I don't believe it myself but I don't have time to think! All I know is there's an eight foot ape stalking my eight point buck! Suddenly the deer bolts. *My* deer – gone! I'm so mad, I look at this big smelly monkey and I yell, "You son-of-a-B!" Damn thing looks at me, steps over a four foot high stump like it's a twig and takes off and I'm thinking, 'Damn, nobody can move that fast in a gorilla suit...That's the real McCoy!' I drop my gun and I take off in the other direction. Now I got no deer, no gun, *and* I owe Dennis an apology for calling him a liar!

(plops down on a log, squirms uncomfortably)

By the way, have you got a clean pair of pants I could borrow?

(They look at him and each other, stunned. Finally **ALICE** *takes the initiative.)*

ALICE. Um, mister deer hunter?

GROVER. *(extending his hand)* Grover. Grover Duffy.

ALICE. *(shaking his hand)* Hi, Grover. Listen, I'm really sorry for your trouble, but we're kind of in the middle of something here, so would you mind leaving?

JESSIE. Alice!

EVAN. Give the guy a break, Alice, he just ran into a sasquatch!

ALICE. Right, but –

*(***EVAN***,* **JESSIE** *and* **GROVER** *speak excitedly, overlapping.)*

EVAN. So that's what that smell was!

JESSIE. I always heard they smelled bad.

GROVER. Dennis told me they were real. I didn't believe him!

JESSIE. Do you think it saw us on the trail?

ALICE. Okay folks, folks, time out. We have to get back to work.

EVAN. *(excited)* Alice, we may have a golden opportunity here. If that sasquatch is still around and we can get it on camera…

ALICE. Evan…please.

EVAN. Please what? How cool would it be to film a bigfoot?!

JESSIE. Every TV station would buy it.

EVAN. I bet some government research center would buy it too!

JESSIE. Yeah!

*(**ALICE** studies them, arms crossed, then lets out a big laugh.)*

ALICE. You guys actually believe in bigfoot?

(laughs more, shakes her head)

That's a good one!

GROVER. Seeing is believing!

ALICE. *(to **GROVER**, gently)* No offense, but it was probably a bear.

GROVER. *(with a vigorous head shake)* I've hunted everything in every province and Alaska too. This was no bear!

EVAN. *(re: **GROVER**)* He seems like a pretty credible guy to me.

ALICE. Listen; even if the sasquatch was real, which it isn't, I'm not out here to find one.

JESSIE. You're not out here to find fifty dollar bills either but if you saw one lying on the ground, wouldn't you pick it up?

EVAN. Come on Alice, you came all this way to make a movie about ghosts -

ALICE. It is *not* a movie! It's a

ALICE & EVAN. multimedia documentary!

EVAN. …Yeah yeah, I know. So make it a documentary about sasquatch.

ALICE. No!

EVAN. Why not?!

ALICE. Because! Hannah…Hannah, help me out. What do you think?

(**HANNAH** *is looking around the woods with apprehension.*)

HANNAH. *(nervously)* Oh, I don't know…channeling apes really isn't my thing. Maybe if they've crossed over to the spirit world.

*(to **GROVER**)*

But you said this one was alive, right?

(**ALICE** *rolls her eyes.*)

ALICE. Okay all you gullible bigfoot believers, let's get back to reality and find some ghosts.

(**ALICE** *takes the EMF from* **HANNAH** *and crosses to the upstage area where the microphone sits. She has her back to the rest of them.*)

ALICE. I'm going to reset the EMF. We've got to get a clear signal.

(The others all wrinkle their noses and make gestures to indicate the bad smell has come back stronger. **GROVER** *suddenly rises, eyes wide, and points to an area offstage above the audience.* **EVAN**, **JESSIE** *and* **HANNAH** *all look too, frozen with fear and awe.)*

ALICE. *(cont.)* We'll let things settle down for a minute because I don't want to pick up any nervous energy from you guys.

(**GROVER** *bolts offstage.* **JESSIE**, **EVAN** *and* **HANNAH** *quickly follow.*)

ALICE. *(cont.) (indicating an upstage area)* Now I figure the center of activity is somewhere around here. Hannah, do you agree? Hannah?

(**ALICE** *turns and is surprised to find herself alone. She steps forward downstage.*)

ALICE. *(cont.)* Hannah? Jessie? Hey, where is everybody?

(holds her nose, reacting to the smell)

ALICE. *(cont.)* Euwww…

*(The EMF in **ALICE**'s hand, which is pointed in the direction where the others were just staring, suddenly starts beeping. **ALICE** looks down at the device, then up over the audience. Her mouth drops open, eyes go wide. An animal grunt is heard followed by the sound of something big crashing through the forest. **ALICE**'s eyes move from one end of the theatre to the other, following it. Sound dies out, brief pause.)*

ALICE. *(cont.) (dull shock)* I just saw a sasquatch.

(pause; with despair –)

No one at Tim Hortons is going to believe me!

(blackout)

End of Play

PROPERTIES LIST

Camcorder
Camera bag
Backpacks (at least four)
Outdoor thermometer
Shoebox
Microphone with long cord
Director's clapboard
Notebook and pen
Hand-held electronic device
Water bottles with water

Little snack bags

COSTUMES

ALICE: Jeans, sweater, scarf, jacket, hiking boots, orange reflector vest

JESSIE: Jeans, long sleeved pullover top, jacket, hiking boots, orange reflector vest

EVAN: Jeans, long sleeved pullover shirt, jacket, orange hunting hat, hiking boots, orange reflector vest

HANNAH: Stylish pants, top and jacket, hiking boots, jewelry

GROVER: Blaze orange hunting pants and jacket, white long sleeved thermal shirt, hunting hat with ear flaps

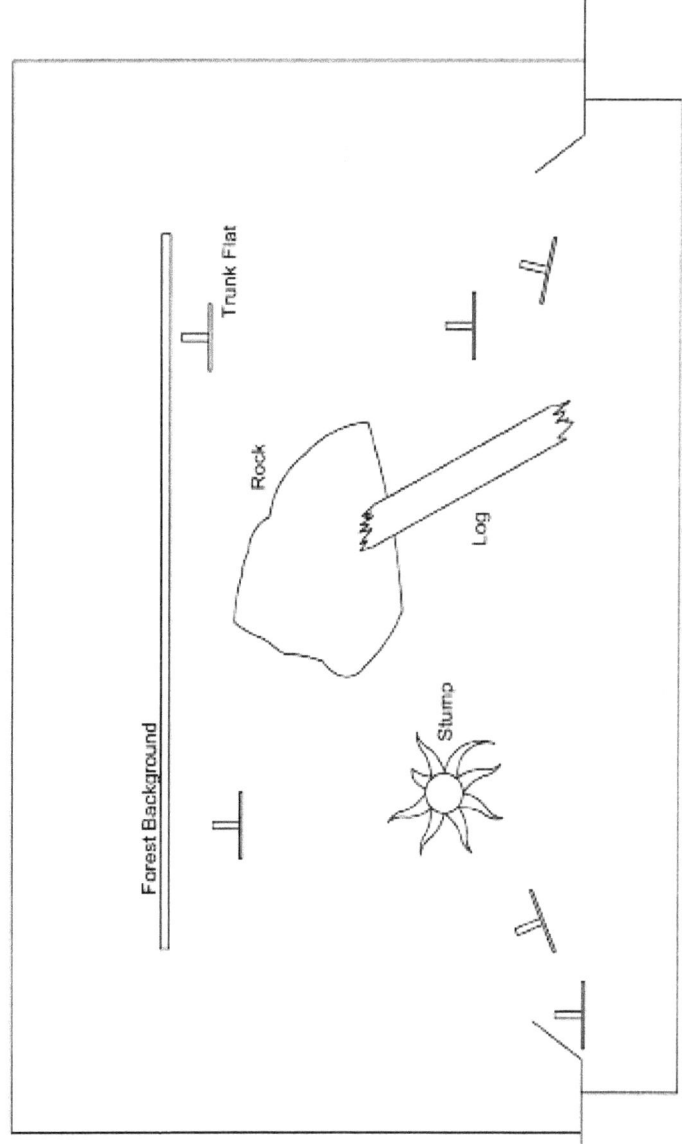

Awesome Ghosts of Ontario
Set Plot by Lowell Olcott

OTHER TITLES AVAILABLE FROM BAKER'S PLAYS

COPIES

Brad Slaight

Dramatic Comedy, Jr. High/High Schools / 2m, 6f

An an orientation camp for new teenage clones, teens are sent to "Camp I.M.U" fresh from the lab to make a transition into the world of the "Originals" who have ordered them made. The newest "Copy" (a word they prefer to "clone") to arrive is a very bright and positive teenager named Michael who soon realizes what the other copies in his cottage have known for awhile – that their stay at the camp is much longer than they had thought. Michael befriends a rebellious Copy named Melissa, who does not get along with her Original and refuses to change her attitude in order to please her. She informs Michael, and the other Copies, that she is going to escape from the camp and fight for what she calls "copy rights". This is a story right out of tomorrow's headlines. Not good at math? Have a clone of yourself made from your own DNA, but gifted in math to do your problems for you. Need a spare part for the future? Your clone is a walking talking parts store. *Copies* explores the heart and soul of clones, bred specifically to do all those things you don't want to do

OTHER TITLES AVAILABLE FROM BAKER'S PLAYS

EYES WIDE OPEN

Jennifer Kirkeby

Drama, High Schools / 2m, 5f

Eyes Wide Open is a touching and informative play about Kristin, a 16 year-old girl who suffers from anorexia and bulimia. Written by a woman who has experienced eating disorders first hand, the story begins after Kristin faints in her dance class. Kristin finds herself in a hospital room where she is met by the spirit of her grandmother, Birdy.

Birdy, who is seen only by Kristin, gently guides her granddaughter through moments of her life. As they revisit the dance studio, Kristin relives both joyful and unhappy experiences with her best friend, Amber. Michael, the boy who Kristin has a crush on, helps her to learn the dance steps. We meet Julia, an obnoxious student who loves to show her "creative" dances and give others fashion advice. Kristin helps Daniel, Michael's younger brother to stop his bad (and dangerous) habit of closing his eyes when he dances. Laura is the dance teacher who tries unsuccessfully to talk to Kristin about her eating disorder. Ultimately, these experiences and Birdy's guidance help Kristin to examine her life and make her final decision whether to live or die.

OTHER TITLES AVAILABLE FROM BAKER'S PLAYS

STAGE KISS

Michael R. Kramer

*Comedy, High School/Community Theatre /
1m, 2f / Simple set*

Kevin and Jill meet during auditions for a community theatre play. Kevin immediately expresses his dismay about the director's decision to have the actors read a kiss scene, with real kissing required. What starts as a debate between two strangers about the wisdom of the director's demands evolves into a funny and fragile connection as two lonely individuals confront their insecurities about romance, sex, and, of course, kissing.

"A story about a cute, romantic tryst"
- *City Edition, Milwaukee*

BAKERSPLAYS.COM

www.ingramcontent.com/pod-product-compliance
Lightning Source LLC
Chambersburg PA
CBHW071846290426
44109CB00017B/1936